Biblos Series

Meetings with Mystery

Theme: Encounter

Sarah Lane

Series Editor: Terence Copley

RMEP

RELIGIOUS AND MORAL EDUCATION PRESS

What is this book about?

This book is about **encounters**, or meetings, that are a mystery or special in some way.

What will I find in this book?

This book contains narratives about five mysterious encounters. The people who had these encounters lived at different times but the narratives all come from the Bible. Some of these people believed their encounters were with God. You will be asked to read these narratives, to think about these encounters and to give your own ideas on questions about mysterious or special encounters.

Why read narratives from the Bible?

The Bible is a collection of books that are important to religious believers who are Jews, Christians or Muslims. For many Jews and Christians, the Bible is very special because they believe it contains God's message for humans.

Do I have to believe in God or the Bible?

For people who are not religious believers, the Bible is still important because of the part it has played in the history of the world.

When you use this book, you will **not** be asked to believe (or disbelieve) in God or in the religions which see the Bible as important. You **will** be asked to **think for yourself** about the questions in the book.

Contents

In this book, you will be asked to think about:

- How some encounters can be puzzling and scary
- What might an encounter with God be like?
- How some encounters can change people's lives
- How can we tell when an encounter we have is different, extra special?

Mysterious and Frightening

In this unit, you will be asked to think about:

- Two narratives about mysterious and frightening events
- What an encounter with God might be like
- How some encounters can be puzzling and scary
- Names and their importance
- The idea of a holy place

Does everything in life always have a simple explanation? What do you think?

I don't know-haven't a clue!

Before you read the narrative below, here are some things you need to know.

Jacob, the son of Isaac, had cheated his twin brother, Esau, out of his inheritance. (You can read about this in the Bible in Genesis 25:19–34 and 27:1–45.) Esau had threatened to kill him. This led Jacob to leave his family for twenty years. At the time we join the narrative, Jacob is on his way back to see his father and brother. He has heard the disturbing news that Esau is on his way to meet him with an army of 400 men. …

A Mysterious Encounter

Jacob got up in the middle of the night and took his wives, his eleven children, and everything he owned across to the other side of the River Jabbok for safety. Afterwards, Jacob went back and spent the rest of the night alone.

A man came and fought with Jacob until just before daybreak. When the man saw that he could not win, he struck Jacob on the hip and threw it out of joint. They kept on wrestling until the man said, "Let go of me! It's almost daylight."

"You can't go until you bless me," Jacob replied.

Then the man asked, "What's your name?"

"Jacob," he answered.

The man said, "Your name will no longer be Jacob. You have wrestled with God and with men, and you have won. That's why your name will be Israel."

Jacob said, "Now tell me your name."

"Don't you know who I am?" he asked. And he blessed Jacob.

Jacob said, "I have seen God face to face, and I am still alive." So he named the place Peniel. The sun was coming up as Jacob was leaving Peniel. He was limping because he had been struck on the hip, and the muscle on his hip joint had been injured.

ADAPTED FROM GENESIS 32:22–32 (CONTEMPORARY ENGLISH VERSION)

Clues

Use these clues to help you answer the questions.

Names

➤ Jacob is an important figure for Jews, Christians and Muslims. His new name, Israel, became the name for a whole people, and today it is the name of a country.

➤ The name 'Jacob' sounds in Hebrew like heel-catcher. This was because he was the second twin to be born and he is said to have grabbed his brother's heel as they were being born (see Genesis 25:19–26).

➤ The name 'Israel' means in Hebrew a man who wrestles with God.

➤ In ancient times, it was believed that if you knew a person's name, you had power over them.

➤ In Arab countries now, babies' names are carefully chosen because of their meaning.

Seeing God's face

➤ The place name 'Peniel' means face of God.

➤ The Bible says in several places that to see God face to face would mean death. It is not clear why, but this may be because God is so powerful and holy (different from anything else in creation) that seeing God's face would be too much for human beings. (One example is Exodus 33:20.)

➤ A blessing was a prayer that God would look after someone and make them successful.

Talk about

1. Why do you think Jacob returned alone across the river in the middle of the night?

2. Why do you think Jacob wanted to be blessed? How might it have helped him?

3. After Jacob's encounter, he had an injured hip that probably hurt for some time, but what might have changed him for ever?

4. In Bible times, if you knew a person's name you were thought to have power over them. What gives people power over each other nowadays? What does it mean if you are on first-name terms with someone?

5. Who was the person who wrestled with Jacob? Think about the reasons for your answer. (*Clue*: Look carefully at the end of the narrative.)

6. What can we learn from mysteries – not detective mysteries, but things in real life that are mysterious?

7. If God is real, will God always be obvious? Why?/Why not?

Make a record

1. This is a very mysterious narrative and it might not all make sense. Read through it again and list all the things you find mysterious or strange about it. Can you think of any explanations for these things or will some of them always be mysterious?

2. Imagine you are Jacob. Write your diary for the night of your strange encounter. Include your reasons for moving your family, your feelings about the possibility of meeting your brother Esau, and your questions and feelings about the mysterious events of the night.

Find out

1. What happened next? Do you think Esau got his revenge? You can read the next part of the narrative in Genesis 33.

2. In Islam, Yakuv (Jacob) is a prophet. Find out more about him in the Qur'an, surahs 2:132–133, 6:84, 18:40, 21:72.

Imagine

1. Jacob's new name tells people he has encountered God and wrestled with him. Think about your own name. Do you know why you were given that name? Do you know what it means? (You could try looking it up at www.behindthename.com) Now try to think of a name for yourself which would tell people about something special that has happened in your life. It doesn't have to sound exactly like a name – for example, you might want to call yourself 'winner of races', 'person who climbed a mountain' or 'smiler'. Write about your reason for choosing this name and the special event that happened to you.

2. Think about some of the things you find mysterious or puzzling, or some of the big questions you have about your life or things that happen in the world. Design a poster showing some of these things. You might like to start by drawing a big question mark in the middle.

   Compare your poster with others in your class/group. Do you all have the same kinds of question? How do we find answers to big questions? Are there some questions that might never have one answer?

Before you read the narrative on the next page, here are some things you need to know.

Mysterious and Frightening 2

- Moses is a very important person in the Hebrew Bible and in the Jewish faith. Muslims know him as Musa, a prophet of Allah (God). This is one of many narratives about him.

- Moses was born at a time when the Hebrews (another name for the Israelites, later called Jews) were slaves in Egypt. Before this narrative begins, he had already escaped death when the Pharaoh, the king of Egypt, had ordered that all Hebrew baby boys were to be killed. Later Moses had fled from Egypt after killing an Egyptian who had been beating a Hebrew slave. He had heard that the Pharaoh wanted to kill him for what he had done. He went to the land of Midian. There he married Zipporah, the daughter of Jethro.

An Encounter on the Hillside

One day, Moses was taking care of the sheep and goats of his father-in-law, Jethro, the priest of Midian. Moses decided to lead them across the desert to Sinai, the holy mountain. There an angel from God appeared to him from a burning bush.

Moses saw that the bush was on fire, but it was not burning up. "This is strange!" he said to himself. "I must go and look at this strange sight and see why the bush isn't burning up." When God saw Moses coming near the bush, God called him by name. Moses answered, "Here I am."

God replied, "Don't come any closer. Take off your sandals – the ground where you are standing is holy. I am the God who was worshipped by your ancestors Abraham, Isaac and Jacob."

Moses was afraid to look at God, so he hid his face.

God said to Moses, "I have seen how the Hebrews, my people, are suffering as slaves in Egypt and I have heard them beg for my help. I have come down to rescue them from the Egyptians. I will bring my people out of Egypt into a country where there is good land, rich with milk and honey. Go to the king, Moses! I am sending you to lead my people out of his country."

But Moses said, "Who am I to go to the king and lead your people out of Egypt?"

God replied, "I will be with you. And you will know that I am the one who sent you, when you worship me on this mountain after you have led my people out of Egypt."

Moses answered, "I will tell the people of Israel that the God their ancestors worshipped has sent me to them. But what should I say if they ask me your name?"

God said to Moses: "I am the eternal God. So tell them that the Lord, whose name is 'I Am', has sent you. This is my name for ever, and it is the name that people must use from now on."

ADAPTED FROM EXODUS 3:1–15 (CONTEMPORARY ENGLISH VERSION)

Use these clues to help you answer the questions on pages 12 and 13.

Clues

➤ Moses became a prophet, which means someone who speaks for God, and a great leader of the Hebrew or Israelite people. The first five books of the Bible – Genesis, Exodus, Leviticus, Numbers and Deuteronomy – make up the Torah, or the Jewish religious law. These books are sometimes called the Books of Moses.

➤ God had promised Abraham that his people would have their own land – the 'promised land' – and this promise is made again to Moses.

➤ The word 'holy' means separate from the ordinary, or special. A holy place is often treated with respect. God tells Moses to take off his sandals as a sign that the place is special and God is present.

➤ The name in Hebrew that God tells Moses is difficult to translate into English but means something like 'I am who I am'. It is sometimes written as 'YHWH'. In Bible times, a name was thought to represent a person. So God's name was thought to tell something about God and was treated with respect. It is not pronounced by Jews, who often read it as 'the Lord' when they see it in writing. In old Bibles it's sometimes written as 'the LORD'.

Thinking it over

Who? Me?

Talk about

1. Why do you think Moses suddenly becomes afraid? How does he react when he first sees the bush? Why do you think he feels like this?

2. How do his feelings change? Why do you think this happens?

3. Why do you think Moses is afraid to look at God? (Think back to the narrative about Jacob on page 5 if you have read it.)

4. Have you ever seen anything really strange and unusual? What was it? How did you feel about it?

5. What job does God give Moses to do?

6. Do you think Moses really wants the job? Why?/Why not?

7. Have you ever been asked to do something really important? Did you do it? How did you feel?

Make a record

1. Imagine you are going to make a film of this narrative. Draw a storyboard (boxes which sketch out what happens in each part of the film) and write the dialogue between Moses and God. Don't spend too long drawing the pictures – sketches will do. Try to limit the words to the most important parts of the story.

2. Think of some words connected with fire, e.g. burn, blaze, flicker, scorch. Make a list of these words, then use them in a poem which describes what Moses saw.

3. This narrative about Moses and his encounter with God often appears in Bible story or picture books for children. Look in your school library for books that include it, then design your own picture book retelling it for younger children. Think carefully about the words you will use and the most helpful pictures. You may like to use a computer to print out your words then add the pictures. Remember that Jews and Muslims do not allow pictures of God.

4. Make a collage representing the burning bush. Use all sorts of different colours and textures. Remember that the bush itself did not burn up. As you do this, think about Moses' reaction to the sight. Is the image of fire powerful? What does it make you think of?

Find out

1. Some religions have holy places today. What kinds of places are they? What makes them special? Find out what you can about some of these places and what religious people do when they visit to show that these places are special.

2. Find out what happens to Moses next by reading Exodus 4:1–20. You will see that Moses has a sort of argument with God. What is it about? Who wins it? What does Moses do as a result? How might he have felt at the end?

3. Why is Moses such an important figure for Jews, Christians and Muslims? Find out by asking any Jews, Christians or Muslims you know, or by using an encyclopedia or web search under Moses.

4. We use the word 'awful' to mean something unpleasant: for example, "Something awful happened to me on the way to school." Using a dictionary, find out what 'awe' means and what 'awe full' originally meant. Then think about whether you would say Jacob's and Moses' experiences were 'awe full'.

Imagine

1. Imagine you are Moses. At the beginning of the narrative you are just looking after the sheep and goats. By the end you have been asked by God to lead the Hebrews out of slavery in Egypt.

   - How would you feel? Look for clues in the narrative.
   - How would you explain this to your family?
   - How would your life have to change?

2. Imagine you have been asked to do something really difficult. What would help you to do what you had been asked? How might a religious person believe God could help them?

3. If God is real, what do you think an encounter with God might be like? Think about these prompt words: pleasant, unpleasant; frightening, comforting; important, unimportant.

   Then try to write a poem in which you use some of the words you have thought up to describe this encounter OR find or compose a piece of music or create a short dance routine that shows the feelings that your words describe.

Someone's Calling My Name!

In this unit, you will be asked to think about:

- How various people's lives were changed as a result of what they believed was an encounter between Samuel and God
- How encounters can change any person's life
- The importance for religious believers of trying to listen for what God is saying
- How, in the narrative, God punishes people after repeated warnings about their repeated wickedness

Can we tell when an encounter in our life is different, extra special? What do you think?

She seems very nice.

How can I help you?

He seems very nice.

I'd like to return this book, please.

Before you read the narrative below, here are some things you need to know.

Samuel had been taken by his mother to the place of worship known as 'God's house' in Shiloh when he was a small child. She left him there to be brought up. She had promised God she would do this and she wanted to show God how grateful she was that God had given her a child. So Samuel lived at Shiloh with Eli, the priest.

A Surprising Encounter

Samuel served God by helping Eli the priest, who was by that time almost blind. In those days, God hardly ever spoke directly to people, and God did not appear to them in dreams very often. But one night, Eli was asleep in his room, and Samuel was sleeping on a mat near the Ark in God's house. They had not been asleep very long when God called out Samuel's name.

"Here I am!" Samuel answered. Then he ran to Eli and said, "Here I am. What do you want?"

"I didn't call you," Eli answered. "Go back to bed."

Samuel went back.

Again God called out Samuel's name. Samuel got up and went to Eli. "Here I am," he said. "What do you want?"

Eli told him, "Son, I didn't call you. Go back to sleep."

God had not spoken to Samuel before, and Samuel did not recognise the voice. When God called out his name for the third time, Samuel went to Eli again and said, "Here I am. What do you want?"

Eli finally realised that it was God who was speaking to Samuel. So he said, "Go back and lie down! If someone speaks to you again, answer, 'I'm listening, Lord. What do you want me to do?'"

Once again Samuel went back and lay down.

God then stood beside Samuel and called out as he had done before, "Samuel! Samuel!"

"I'm listening," Samuel answered. "What do you want me to do?"

God said: "Samuel, I am going to do something in Israel that will shock everyone who hears about it! Their ears will tingle! I will punish Eli and his family, just as I promised. His sons have been blaspheming me and he has done nothing to stop them. He has let them get away with it, even though I warned him I would punish his family for ever. I told Eli that sacrifices or offerings could never make things right! His family has gone too far."

The next morning, Samuel got up and opened the doors to God's house. He was afraid to tell Eli what God had said. But Eli told him, "Samuel, my boy, come here!"

"Here I am," Samuel answered.

Eli said, "What did God say to you? Tell me everything. I pray that God will punish you terribly if you don't tell me every word he said!"

So Samuel told Eli everything. Then Eli said, "He is the Lord, and he will do what is right."

As Samuel grew up, God spoke to him again and again and made everything Samuel said come true. Everyone in the country knew that Samuel was truly God's prophet. God often appeared to Samuel at Shiloh to tell him what to say. After that, Samuel would speak to the whole nation of Israel.

1 Samuel 3:1–4:1 (adapted from the Contemporary English Version)

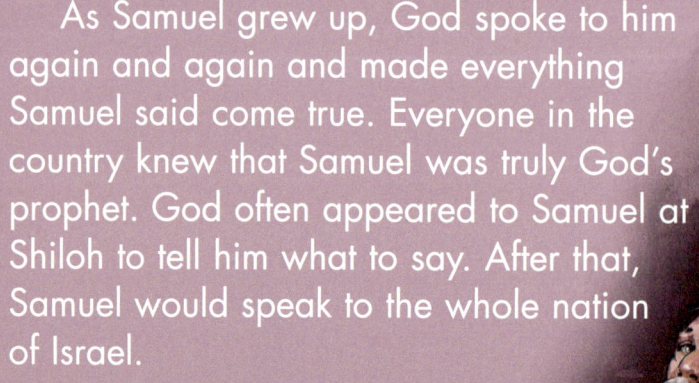

➤ We know how important Samuel was because of the books in the Bible which are named after him. These tell what happened to him.

➤ It is not known how old Samuel was when the events in this narrative happened, but he was still a child.

➤ Sometimes children were given as a thank offering to God and allowed to live away from their parents and grow up in a 'house of God' or temple.

➤ Samuel became a very important prophet. Some people think that a prophet is someone who speaks about what is going to happen in the future, but in the Bible (and the Qur'an) a prophet is someone who gives the people messages from God.

➤ The Ark was a box believed to hold the stones on which the Ten Commandments were first written. It was kept in the Shiloh Temple. (Earlier in the Bible, the same word is used for Noah's ark, which was a box-shaped boat.)

➤ Priests led worship and carried out animal sacrifices as well as looking after God's house. Sacrifices usually cost a lot and were not easy to do – only the best animals could be offered. Sacrifices were offered to thank God or sometimes to say sorry for something that someone had done.

➤ The word 'blasphemy' comes from a Greek word meaning really abusive language. Blasphemy is language directly attacking God. Not believing in God is not blasphemy but the use of hateful, attacking language or curses against God would be seen as blasphemy. Blasphemy is still against the law in many countries, including the UK, although in Britain court cases are very rare.

Use these clues to help you answer the questions on pages 18 and 19.

Guilty!

Thinking it over

Talk about

1. Why do you think Samuel didn't realise God was speaking to him?

2. Do you think Samuel heard the voice inside, or was it an 'outside' voice like a parent's or teacher's? Say why.

3. How might someone recognise God's voice or believe that God was speaking to them?

4. Why do you think Samuel was chosen to be God's messenger to Eli?

5. Do you think Samuel's age made it easier or more difficult for him to give God's message to Eli? Would an older person have been a better choice?

6. Do you think it was right of Eli to try to force Samuel to tell him the message – after all, it could have been private? Why?/Why not?

7. Why might people's ears have tingled when they heard the message?

8. Have you ever had to pass on some bad or difficult news? How did you feel? How would you tell someone something you know they won't like?

9. Should parents be blamed for their children's behaviour? Up to a certain age of the child? Or for ever? Give reasons for your answer.

10. If God is real, do you think God ever punishes people? Why?/ Why not?

11. Eli's family is to be punished by God for blasphemy. Do you think God was right to punish Eli's family for repeated offences that Eli had done nothing to prevent? Why?/Why not?

12. Do you sometimes feel that adults don't listen to children enough? Are there things that children can say better than adults? What might they be?

13. Samuel obeys God when God calls. Give examples of people we should obey and when. Is it ever right to disobey people? In what sorts of situation?

14. Are people good listeners? How important is it to listen to the people we meet?

15. If God is real, how might we 'hear' God's voice?

Make a record

1. Imagine you are Samuel. Write a letter to your mother, Hannah, and your father, Elkanah, telling them what happened to you and how God spoke to you. Don't forget to include your thoughts and feelings.

2. If Eli kept a diary, what might he have written in it at the end of the day after all this happened? Concentrate on his feelings rather than just the events.

3. Imagine one of Eli's sons visits him on the day after this happened. Script their conversation like a play. Do they each blame the other for the punishment that they will suffer? Is the son sorry or defiant?

Find out

1. Find out more about prophets. Find out the names of some other prophets in the Bible and what they are asked to say and do.

2. In Islam there is a line of prophets from Prophet Adam to Prophet Muhammad (pbuh). Find out the names of as many as you can.

3. Read about what happened after this in 1 Samuel 4:2–22, about the battle of Shiloh and the death of Eli. What do you think the writer believed these events showed about God? Why did the writer think that Ichabod was such a good name for the baby?

4. Talk to some religious believers and ask them how they feel God communicates with them. Share your research with the rest of the class. Make a chart to display your findings.

5. Find out about Quaker meetings. They begin with a shared silence in which people try to listen together for the 'leadings' or message of God.

Imagine

1. Samuel may have been aged 7–11 or a little older at the time of this encounter. Imagine you are Samuel. You are lying on your mat in the house of God after hearing God's message and wondering: should I tell Eli? All of it? A bit of it? How will he react? Script your thoughts.

2. Imagine you were hiding in God's house when all this happened. What would you have seen and heard? Write a script for a conversation you might have if you told someone about what had happened. Try to imagine the questions they might ask you and the answers you would give.

3. Have you ever had an experience that has changed your life? What difference did it make? If you had an experience in which you believed you heard God's voice, how would you feel about it?

Close Enough to Touch

Seeing is believing – or is it? What do you think?

In this unit, you will be asked to think about:

- The Christian belief that Jesus was raised from the dead and that he appeared to his friends and followers
- The idea that we don't always see things about people we know very well
- What angels might be like

It WAS her!

- This is part of a long and very important narrative for Christians. It explains that Jesus was sentenced to death by being crucified (hung on a wooden cross) and was buried in a cave-tomb with a rock across the front.

- When his two of his disciples (friends and followers) went with a woman called Mary Magdalene to Jesus' tomb two days later, they discovered that the tomb was open and Jesus' body was no longer there. The two men ran back to tell the others what had happened and this is where Mary Magdalene's story begins.

- Jesus died on a Friday and was buried the same day. The Sabbath, the Jewish holy day (from sunset on Friday to sunset on Saturday) started a few hours after Jesus' death, so Sunday morning was the first opportunity anyone had to visit the tomb. One of the Jewish Ten Commandments forbids work on the Sabbath. This probably meant that Jesus' friends did not have time to prepare his body for burial as well as they would have liked to, as this would have counted as work.

Before you read the narrative on the next page, here are some things you need to know.

Friday

Jesus dies and is hurriedly buried.

Saturday

SABBATH
All work forbidden

Sunday

Early in morning, two disciples and Mary Magdalene visit the tomb.

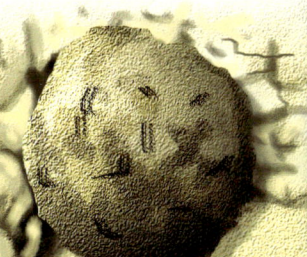

An Encounter with an Old Friend

Mary Magdalene stood crying outside the tomb. She was still weeping when she stooped down and saw two angels inside. They were dressed in white and were sitting where Jesus' body had been. One was at the head and the other was at the foot. The angels asked Mary, "Why are you crying?"

She answered, "They have taken away Jesus' body! I don't know where they have put him."

As soon as Mary said this, she turned around and saw Jesus standing there. But she did not recognise him. Jesus asked her, "Why are you crying? Who are you looking for?"

She thought he was the gardener and said, "Sir, if you have taken his body away, please tell me, so I can go and get him."

Then Jesus said to her, "Mary!"

She turned and said to him, "Teacher."

Jesus said to her, "Don't hold on to me! I have not yet gone to the Father. But tell my disciples that I am going to the one who is my Father and my God, as well as your Father and your God." Mary Magdalene then went and told the disciples that she had seen Jesus. She also told them what he had said to her.

ADAPTED FROM THE GOSPEL OF JOHN 20:11–18 (CONTEMPORARY ENGLISH VERSION)

Clues

Use these clues to help you answer the questions.

➤ Mary was probably visiting the tomb to finish putting ointments and herbs and spices on Jesus' body, because this 'work' had been interrupted by the start of the Sabbath.

➤ The Hebrew word Mary uses when she recognises Jesus is 'Rabboni', which means teacher. Jewish religious teachers are now called 'Rabbi'.

➤ The word 'angel' means messenger. In the Bible, angels are sometimes human beings who are bringing God's message, but sometimes heavenly creatures. Angels often appear when something dramatic is going to happen. In Luke's Gospel, an angel comes to tell a different Mary that she will be the mother of Jesus (see Luke 1:26–38).

Talk about

1. Why was the tomb empty? What explanations could there have been for this? What might have happened to Jesus' body?

2. What do Christians believe happened?

3. What do you think about the idea that someone could be raised from the dead?

4. The narrative says that Mary saw two angels inside the tomb. How do you think she knew they were angels? What is an angel? What do you think they might look like?

5. What kinds of things sometimes make it difficult for us to recognise people we know? Have you ever walked past someone you know and not noticed them? If so, how did it happen?

6. Why do you think Mary didn't recognise Jesus when she saw him? How do you think she felt when she did recognise him?

7. In Jesus' time, women were not thought to be reliable witnesses and were not asked to be official witnesses. In this narrative, the writer of John's Gospel shows Mary Magdalene as the first witness who sees Jesus when he has risen from death. What makes a good witness? Would Mary have made a good witness? Why?/Why not? Do you think it might have made any difference that Jesus' first appearance was to a woman?

8. Why do you think this narrative is so important for Christians? What does it tell Christians about Jesus? What does it tell Christians about God?

Oh no – Mum will *go* mad!

9. Have you ever had an experience that was so surprising or unusual that you thought other people might not believe you? If something like that happened to you, how would you convince people that you were telling the truth?

10. Jesus gave Mary a message for the disciples. What is the most important thing you have ever had to tell anyone? How did you feel when you had to tell them?

11. Are the thoughts and actions of people we know well predictable? Do they often do what we expect them to do? Can you predict how someone you know will behave in a certain situation? (*Example*: A parent if you lose something expensive on the way home from school.)

12. Have you ever been surprised when someone you know well has acted in an unpredictable way? What did you learn from that experience?

Make a record

1. Look for clues in the narrative about the way Mary's feelings change. Find each place where you think she might be feeling something different and make a note of it. Draw pictures to show Mary's expressions. Try to show in your pictures the changes in Mary's feelings. Then write a sentence or two to describe the changes in words.

2. Carry on the narrative from where it ends. What happens when Mary tells the disciples what she has seen? Start with this sentence: "Mary burst into the room, breathless and struggling to get the words out…"

Find out

1. Read what the gospels say about Jesus appearing to other people. Jesus' disciple Thomas (often nicknamed 'doubting Thomas') said that he would not believe Jesus had risen unless he could touch the wounds in Jesus' hands and sides. You can read about him in John 20:24–29. Was Thomas right to be doubtful? Do you believe something only if you can see and touch some evidence? Would it be easier to believe in God if you could see and touch God?

2. In John 21:1–14, Jesus goes on a fishing trip and then eats breakfast with his disciples. Why do you think Christians believe this narrative is important? Why is it important for Christians to show that Jesus was real and solid, and not a ghost, after he was raised from death?

3. There is another narrative where Jesus is not recognised straight away, in Luke's Gospel (24:13–35). It tells of two disciples who meet Jesus, after his resurrection, on the way to a place called Emmaus. At what point do they discover his identity?

4. Jews and Muslims believe in angels, as do some Christians. Find out about the angel Gabriel in the Jewish religion and in Islam, where he is called Jibril.

Imagine

1. Imagine the narrative ended with the tomb empty but no other evidence of Jesus. What difference might this have made to what Christians believe today? Would there be any Christians if it had happened like that?

2. Imagine you have the opportunity to interview Mary Magdalene on television. What questions would you ask her? What do you think her answers would be? Explore how she felt when she discovered that she had been the first person to see Jesus. Was she surprised that Jesus chose her? Act out your interview.

3. Imagine you were the real gardener there in the garden. What would you have seen? Draw a picture or make a model to show the scene in the garden. Concentrate especially on the faces and expressions of the people in the scene.

About Turn!

In this unit, you will be asked to think about:

- How Saul's life changed as a result of what he believed was an encounter with Jesus

- How dramatic encounters can change a person's attitudes

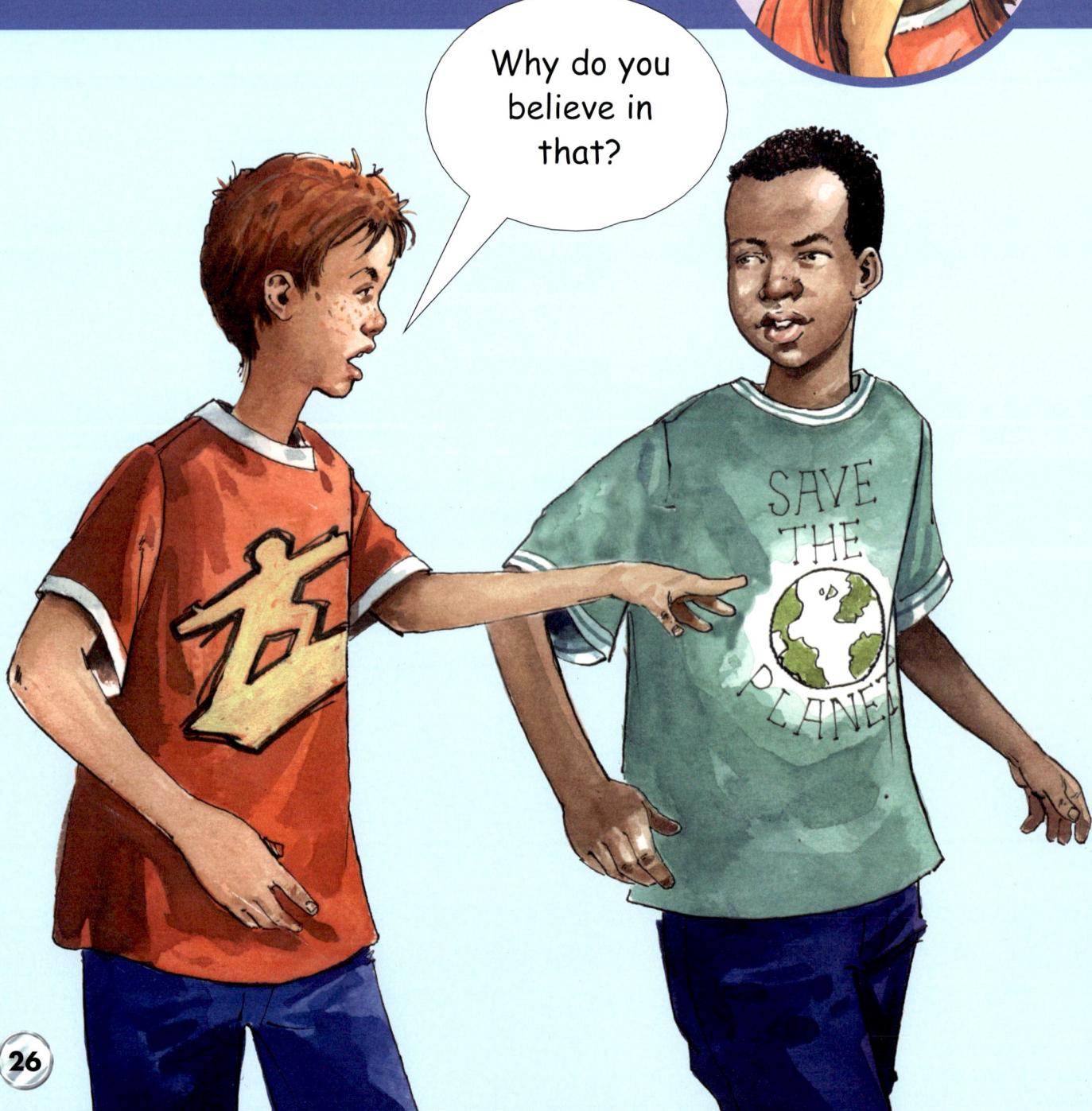

How do we acquire (get) our key beliefs and attitudes?

Why do you believe in that?

Before you read the narrative below, here are some things you need to know.

- This narrative comes from the Book of The Acts of the Apostles (Acts for short) in the Christian New Testament. Acts was written by the same person who wrote the Gospel of Luke.

- Acts is about the first Christians in the early years after Jesus' death and resurrection. To begin with, Christians were all Jews and were seen as part of the Jewish faith, not, like now, as following a completely separate religion. Two main beliefs made them different from other Jews:

  1. They believed that Jesus was the Son of God, or the Messiah, for whom the other Jews were still waiting.

  2. They believed that God had raised Jesus from the dead.

- The nickname 'Christian' had not even been given to the followers of Jesus at the time when the events in this narrative happened.

A Dramatic Encounter

Saul was still breathing threats and murder against Jesus' followers. He even went to the High Priest in Jerusalem and asked for letters to the Jewish leaders in Damascus. He did this because he wanted to arrest and take to the Jewish authorities in Jerusalem any man or woman who had accepted Christianity, so that they could be punished.

When Saul had almost reached Damascus, a bright light from heaven suddenly flashed around him. He fell to the ground and heard a voice that said, "Saul, Saul! Why are you so cruel to me?"

"Who are you?" Saul asked.

"I am Jesus," the voice answered. "I am the one you are so cruel to. Now get up and go into the city, where you will be told what to do."

The men with Saul stood there speechless. They had heard the voice, but they had not seen anyone. Saul got up from the ground, and when he opened his eyes, he could not see a thing. Someone then led him by the hand to Damascus, and for three days he was blind and did not eat or drink.

ACTS 9:1–9 (ADAPTED FROM CONTEMPORARY ENGLISH VERSION)

Clues

Use these clues to help you answer the questions.

➤ At this time, people who followed Jesus were thought of as troublemakers. Jesus had been put to death on the charge of treason (plotting against the Roman Empire) and his followers were seen as people who might cause trouble for the Jewish and Roman authorities.

➤ There was a lot of conflict between the Jews who followed Jesus and the Jews who did not. Most Jews thought the claim that Jesus was the Son of God, the Messiah they were waiting for, was false. Some saw Jesus' followers as not only wrong but dangerous – they could do a lot of damage to the Jewish faith by spreading false claims about God's Son and must be stopped.

➤ Acts mentions Saul earlier on (Acts 8:3) as someone who 'started making a lot of trouble for the Church. He went from house to house, arresting men and women and putting them in jail.' Here 'Church' means the people who followed Jesus. (This word is still used for groups of Christians, as well as buildings where Christians worship.)

➤ Damascus was the most important city in Syria. Many Jews lived there. The people Saul was going to arrest were probably Jewish Christians who had fled to Damascus from Jerusalem, where they were being persecuted.

➤ After this encounter Saul is more often called by his Roman name Paul. There is a King Saul in the Old Testament/Hebrew Bible, but the two Sauls are not the same person, and lived more than 1000 years apart in time.

➤ Saul went on to become one of the most famous Christians and travelled far and wide to tell people about Jesus. He is also well known for the letters he wrote to Churches in different places, to advise and help them. Some of these letters are found in the New Testament.

➤ Some Christians were very suspicious about Saul's sudden conversion – had he really changed from being their enemy and become a follower of Jesus? Not surprisingly, they were wary about meeting him.

Talk about

1. How was Saul 'cruel' to Jesus?

2. Before this encounter, Saul must have known a lot about the claims being made about Jesus. Acts (9:21) says he was already known in Damascus as 'the man who made havoc in Jerusalem' among Jesus' followers. What do you think Saul 'breathing threats and murder' against the followers of Jesus shows about his feelings? Why might he have felt so strongly? Use the clues to support your answer.

3. Sometimes bullies are frightened people inside and their violence comes from a sort of fear. Is that true of any bullies you have known? Are violent people really scared people who try to scare others to hide their own fears?

4. Do you think Saul might have been afraid of Jesus? What if, deep down, he felt the claims about Jesus were right and he was wrong?

5. Why do you think Jesus chose to speak to Saul? Was he an obvious choice as a leader for Jesus' followers?

6. Why do you think Saul obeyed the voice? How was he so sure that it was Jesus speaking to him? (*Possible cue words:* confusion, shock, certainty.)

7. Do you think it helped that the people with Saul heard the voice too? Would Saul have believed the voice if he had been the only one who heard it? What might he have thought was happening in that case?

8. How did Saul's life change as a result of this experience? Do you think this could be said to be the most important thing that ever happened to Saul? Why?/Why not?

9. What is the most important thing that has ever happened to you? Explain why.

Make a record

1. This encounter was witnessed by the people with Saul. Write a newspaper report about it for the *Damascus Times*. Include interviews with the witnesses and with Saul. You might find it easiest to work as a group and each concentrate on a separate piece of the report. You could produce your report on a computer and design the whole front page with a suitable banner headline.

OR

2. Draw a strip-cartoon which illustrates Saul's encounter. Choose the most important parts of the narrative and write a caption for each picture.

OR

3. Imagine you were present when this encounter took place. In a group, decide who will act as each person in the narrative. Position yourselves as you imagine Saul and those with him may have looked on the road to Damascus. Think about how you would have reacted to the voice and to what happened to Saul. Freeze the scene at the moment the voice is heard. Concentrate on your reactions, your position in the scene and the expression on your face. If you have a camera available, your teacher could take a photograph or video and you could compare your scene with others.

4. You are a composer and you are going to write a piece of music based on this narrative. Using the instruments you have in school and working with others, try to decide what kinds of sound you would use to represent Saul before his dramatic encounter with Jesus, and then how he felt afterwards. What sounds would you use for Jesus' voice and for the bright light? Try to retell the narrative using the sounds you have chosen. You will need to decide which parts of the narrative need to have different sounds – it may help to make a list before you start using instruments.

Find out

1. Read what happened next in Acts 9:10–19.

2. What do people mean when they talk about 'a Damascus Road experience' today? Why do you think people still use this phrase?

3. Read what Saul (now called Paul) himself says about this encounter in Galatians 1:13–17. What are the main differences between his account and Luke's?

Imagine

1. Imagine you are planning your life in a particular way (job, family, place to live, etc.) and then an encounter happens that changes it completely. What sort of encounter do you think would do that? How might it change your plans? Would you be pleased?

2. Imagine you are a Damascus Christian whose brother or sister in Jerusalem has been attacked and beaten up for their beliefs by people who Saul had stirred up. How might you feel when you heard about his conversion, how he had changed? Would you be prepared to meet him? Why?/Why not? What would you want to say to him if you did meet him?

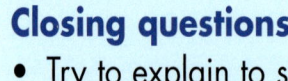

Closing questions

- Try to explain to someone else how an encounter might change a person's life.
- Which of the encounters in the narratives in this book was the most surprising? Why?
- In what ways did some of the people in this book feel that they had met God?
- Do you agree with them? Why?/Why not?

Religious and Moral Education Press
A division of SCM-Canterbury Press Ltd
A wholly owned subsidiary of Hymns Ancient & Modern Ltd
St Mary's Works, St Mary's Plain
Norwich, Norfolk NR3 3BH

First published 2005

ISBN 1 85175 280 3

Designed and typeset by TOPICS – The Creative Partnership, Exeter

Illustrations by Jeff Anderson and Diann Timms

Printed in Great Britain by Brightsea Press, Exeter for SCM-Canterbury Press Ltd, Norwich